ABANDONED NORTH TEXAS

ABANDONED
NORTH TEXAS

SHANE AND JESSICA STEEVES

AMERICA
THROUGH TIME®
ADDING COLOR TO AMERICAN HISTORY

America Through Time is an imprint of Fonthill Media LLC
www.through-time.com
office@through-time.com

Published by Arcadia Publishing by arrangement with Fonthill Media LLC
For all general information, please contact Arcadia Publishing:
Telephone: 843-853-2070
Fax: 843-853-0044
E-mail: sales@arcadiapublishing.com
For customer service and orders:
Toll-Free 1-888-313-2665

www.arcadiapublishing.com

First published 2019

ISBN 978-1-63499-125-4

Typeset in Trade Gothic 10pt on 15pt
Printed and bound in England

CONTENTS

ABOUT THE AUTHORS

Shane and Jessica Steeves met in Colorado sometime in the late 90s. Since then, they have moved to Texas, purchased a house, gotten married, and started a family. More than a decade ago, Shane was surfing the web and came across an image of an old hotel in Mineral Wells that peaked his interest. A few months later, the two were privileged enough to explore the hotel. This started the pair's obsession with abandoned buildings, photography, and architecture. Having previous backgrounds in photography, this became an all-consuming hobby they both can enjoy together.

Shane and Jessica Steeves

INTRODUCTION

For over the last decade, both of us have been obsessed with searching out and exploring historic and abandoned locations. This is especially true for the big state of Texas. What developed as a side hobby, quickly evolved into a passion for photography, architecture, and history. We have explored abandoned and forbidden places most of our lives. Growing up in the Midwest exposed us to locations such as gold mines and abandoned farms, as well as subterranean tunnels.

After about a decade of living in Texas, we started to see images of beautiful buildings that were just being left alone to rot. This rekindled our interest for these long forgotten, neglected places. Shortly after getting back into it, we discovered photographs taken by Dallas based photographer Noel Kerns, which definitely added fuel to the fire. The two of us started out shooting purely documentary style. After taking Noel's light painting workshop, we were able to utilize this method to start creating images with more of a fine art feel. Since then, our lives have begun to revolve around these abandoned buildings and our next chance to photograph them.

It has always amazed us how these spectacular properties can just sit open in plain view while everyone else chooses to dismiss them. Most people just don't see the beauty in them like we do. One of our favorite things is to witness nature reclaiming a location. There is nothing that quite compares to the smell of sheet rock, insulation, and decaying wood.

Many people don't understand the process that goes into finding these forgotten places. Countless hours are spent staring at the map and even more hours are spent driving to locations to see if they are accessible or even worth photographing. We have run into almost every situation imaginable. Drug addicts, scrappers, gang members, and bums are not uncommon to run into in the dark shadows.

Since exploring has recently become so popular with the younger generation, some of these shady characters have been seeking them out and targeting them for their photo gear. The new generation of explorers don't really see how dangerous these locations can be. It is also important to keep in mind the reason each building was closed. It could be anything from lack of funding, to fire, collapse, asbestos, a hoarding situation, death, chemical contamination, or sometimes black mold. We don't recommend trespassing and would never encourage breaking the law. We continuously get permission to photograph these locations from property owners, fire marshals, local police, and lead contractors on construction sites. Over the years, we have seen people get arrested, injured, robbed, and a few have died doing what they loved. We do not recommend this to anyone! Please feel free to check out more of our work at www.facebook.com/decayedandabandonedtexas, www.decayedandabandonedtexas.com, or on Instagram @fatwax4 or @squishesound.

1

CHURCHES

St. John's Catholic Church in West Texas was built in 1936. The building resides on a private farm. The owners of this church used to allow visitors inside, but due to vandalism and ghost hunters, occasionally it can be locked up tight.

Religion is a big deal here in the Lone Star State. There are over six million registered churches in every denomination imaginable. Texas is notorious for their stadium-size churches and their devoted followers. Everything from cults to televangelists can be found preaching their gospel. Churches run rampant here in the South, residing on almost every corner.

Often towns that are too small to have a general store or even a school will still have a place for worship. With such a surplus of Texas churches, many of them are left abandoned. Sometimes, but not often, the stained-glass windows are still in one piece and empty pews still sit scattered across the rooms. Out-of-tune pianos can usually be found collecting dust and cobwebs. Altars, baptismal pools, pulpits, and also wasp nests are all too common to run into. On rare occasions, bats and drug paraphernalia can also be found in the buildings.

The altar from the long-abandoned St. John's church in West Texas.

As churches are prepped for demolition or remodeling, the pews are sometimes moved and gathered up in back rooms. These were left in the back room, where the only available light shines through the stained glass.

The most common things found in churches are pianos. This instrument was found in the attic of a church that was also inhabited by racoons. You can see the tiny pawprints on the face of the piano.

Schulz Co.
CHICAGO
OOK, MAYS & CO.
ALLAS, TEXAS

A small number of these churches still have their stained-glass windows intact. Unfortunately, the majority of the time, these pieces of artwork have been destroyed by vandals.

The room where the Tabernacle would be kept and prepared.

This shot is from the altar of the largest church we have photographed so far.

There is a tremendous amount of seating leading up to the altar in this huge East Texas small-town church.

Balcony seating lit up with the glow of stained glass.

Often stained glass will have bible verses, names of saints, and sometimes dedications to members of the congregation.

This chair sits undisturbed by a broken stained-glass window.

The choir seating area is now home to a colony of bats.

Bats covered the ceiling of this tiny church in the ghost town of Silver, Texas.

The choir stall and baptismal pool area in the small ghost town church.

Bibles and prayer hymns normally litter the floors.

A worm's eye view of a beautiful Catholic church.

Soon after this image was taken, this church was vandalized and most of the stained glass had been removed. We are not quite sure if the owner was trying to salvage them or if vandals had stolen them.

This picture of the altar of a church in Jermyn was obviously staged. This spot is so well known, people regularly stage their photos with items found in the church.

The pews of this church are falling through the sketchy floor after the roof collapsed on them.

This simple church was surprisingly not vandalized when we checked it out. Located in a run-down neighborhood in Ft. Worth, all of the other rooms besides the chapel had been destroyed.

Colorful stained glass in a Ft. Worth church.

Stained glass from the Weber Funeral Home in the DFW area. This property is located in a rough part of town. After stumbling upon somebody's stash of illicit drugs, we quickly left the building. Shortly after our visit a fire was set, and the structure was demolished a few months later.

2

HOTELS

A towering hotel in the city of Texarkana.

Abandoned hotels are scattered throughout the massive state of Texas. Even in their state of disrepair, some of them remain historic southern landmarks. Many of them have been left over from local industries in the area dying out. This generally leaves the town's businesses, hotels, and schools to slowly decline and decay.

In a large majority of these unoccupied buildings, there are remnants of the past left behind. These old phones were discovered in the lobby of an old hotel in Northwest Texas.

Undisclosed historic hotel from the 1800s with original furniture, drapes, and wallpaper.

Some places are purposefully staged by historic societies to show examples of their former glory. Unfortunately, vandals and thieves typically make them regret that decision. Thankfully this place has been locked up tight to preserve the history that remains inside the walls.

One of the former grand staircases in the Cadillac Hotel in Greeneville, Texas.

A once used, now oxidized, elevator.

The lobby of the Cadillac Hotel in Greenville. There isn't much left of this once stunning hotel.

Grand staircases, like this, are ordinarily found in the larger long-forgotten hotels.

This captivating lobby belongs to the Hotel Grim, which was the crown jewel of the city. It is set to be repurposed into lofts and apartments.

The mezzanine of the Hotel Grim. This was a small room on the second floor.

Upstairs above the lobby has a nice view of the room down below.

Peeling paint can be found in every room.

The natural decay in the building adds texture to everything and gives it a unique feel.

This tired, old, lonely chair sits after years of being deserted.

The original hotel furniture is often left behind when the doors close for business. This couch sits slowly deteriorating in a small room here.

A former quaint hotel in Tyler, Texas.

This structure is severely damaged. Heavily scrapped and defaced, it's hardly recognizable.

The formerly abandoned Statler Hotel is located in downtown Dallas. This happened to be the first Hilton Hotel in the city and was an icon for decades.

The decorative glass bar wall that remained in the Statler before it was renovated.

Exterior fisheye shot of the Baker Hotel.

THE BAKER HOTEL

The most iconic abandonment in Texas is the grand Baker Hotel. Nestled in downtown Mineral Wells, it towers over the rest of the buildings in the city. Built in 1929 by Wyatt C. Hendrick, it catered to the rich and famous at the time. This behemoth hotel was a spa destination in the late twenties. The Baker was commissioned by T. B. Baker, who was the original owner of the hotel. Unfortunately, he had to claim bankruptcy in the mid-1930s. After that, he handed control over to his nephew Earl Baker.

Although it opened near the depression, the Baker Hotel continued to be a successful retreat destination. A-list celebrities such as Clark Gable, Bonnie and Clyde, LBJ, the Three Stooges and Judy Garland were among some of the guests. The massive hotel boasted 450 guest rooms, a grand lobby, an Olympic size pool, and even a ballroom in the sky.

The hotel was built in the tiny town of Mineral Wells because of the overabundance of local mineral spring water. In the 30s, people thought the water had medicinal qualities. Many would come from all around to treat anything from headaches to cancer. The hotel was open for thirty years before the first time it closed its doors in 1963. In 1965, local investors were able to lease the hotel from the family. The property suffered years of decline. Then came the fatal heart attack of Earl Baker in the Baker suite in 1967. The Baker Hotel finally closed its doors to the public in 1972.

Since then, a number of groups have talked about the renovation of the Baker Hotel. Sadly, it seems to end in failure every time. The city of Mineral Wells has even implemented a tax to try to offset the millions of dollars needed for renovations. The lobby has been cleaned up recently with viewing windows added to accommodate walking tours.

This hotel single handedly started our obsession with abandoned buildings. Over the past decade, we have literally watched the building being ripped apart by scrappers, teenagers, vandals, adventure seekers, and ghost hunters. It is by far the most well-known and supposedly the most haunted abandonment in the state of Texas.

A few relics of the past still remain in the basement. Ancient kitchen equipment, laundry equipment, and other random items are scattered along this floor. According to urban legend, this is where a bellboy was crushed by a service elevator and died a few days later.

The Baker's lobby was one of the most magnificent in the nation, but after years of decay it has been left in a moldy and derelict state.

The once glamourous spa now sits deteriorating from years of neglect and miscreants.

The spa room is on the second floor and still has a great deal of equipment left behind from its years of service.

It is rumored that Bonnie and Clyde stayed in this room while they were in town.

This Murphy bed is in one of the upper rooms where signs of the original hotel still remain.

The first shot of the Dead Boys Room is from 2008. The second is from ten years later.

The Baker stairs started a true obsession of staircases for one of us. At times risking his life and camera for the perfect shot. This was a private set of stairs coming off of the Baker suite leading to the lobby.

The wealthier guests of the Baker were privileged enough to stay in these larger, more ornate suites.

Mr. Baker's suite has exquisite woodworking. The details in this room are exceptionally intricate compared to the rest of the hotel. Included is a hidden liquor cabinet that was used during prohibition in the 1920s all the way to 1933.

The main set of elevator doors that lead from the lobby to the top floor's Cloud Room.

Arches leading from the elevators to the Cloud Room provided a grand entrance to the ballroom.

The Baker has a beautiful ballroom on the top floor known as the Cloud Room. Even after decades of neglect there is still a beauty to be found when stepping onto this floor overlooking the downtown Mineral Wells area.

A fisheye view halfway onto The Baker's balcony.

We are not 100% sure if there was ever a bell in the bell tower, but what an amazing view.

3

HOSPITALS

Vacant hospital on the border of Texas and Oklahoma.

Every major city or town will have a medical center or hospital located within. The needs of these cities are constantly changing with the evolution or decline of these areas. New hospitals are frequently built while neighboring ones are closed. More often than not, we find derelict equipment and other medical paraphernalia left in otherwise empty rooms. These items can range anywhere from blood samples to x-rays and even operating equipment.

This recently closed hospital in Denison, Texas, was built in 1965. The power had been left on for at least a year after its closure. Different alarms in every part of the building were going off. Much to our surprise, even the automated doors opened.

Crutches left behind in the basement of a vacant hospital.

The nurses' station in an intensive care unit.

The emergency ambulance entrance.

The balcony view of an empty hospital in North Texas.

An equipment control panel that once served a purpose.

Depending on the size of the hospital, some can seem more like a maze, especially in the basement.

It's a regular occurrence to find rusty beds.

The supply room from a military hospital.

A dark corridor that leads to the patient's rooms in the Nazareth Hospital.

The staircase from the Nazareth Hospital in Mineral Wells.

Eventually, if left abandoned long enough, these buildings face the fate of being burnt to the ground, filled with trash, or vandalized.

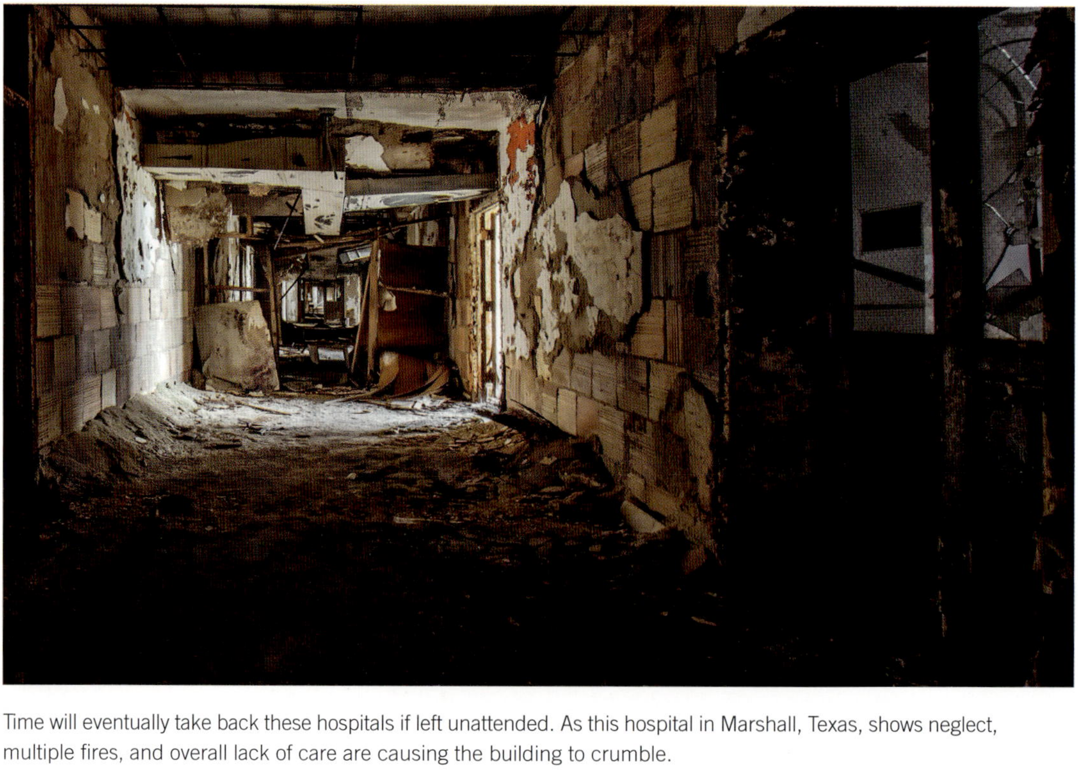

Time will eventually take back these hospitals if left unattended. As this hospital in Marshall, Texas, shows neglect, multiple fires, and overall lack of care are causing the building to crumble.

The main staircase of the Railroad Hospital in Marshall, Texas.

A lonely chair sits at the back of a covered path, left to the elements, outside of the Railroad Hospital.

A dead-end hallway in a retirement hospital in Whitewright.

A small hospital located in Terrell has an eerie blue glow from window tint and paint. This is the main nurses' station of the hospital.

The Terrell Hospital's main corridor leading to the patient's rooms.

Exterior shot of the now demolished Palestine Hospital.

Palestine Hospital

One of our favorite hospitals was an old building in the city of Palestine, Texas. It existed as an unknown spot for quite a while. Many of the hospital's relics still lingered around. Amidst all of the hospital equipment and supplies, we were able to find blood samples, incubators, medical slides, as well as records and x-rays from when the infirmary was still open.

The Palestine Hospital was built sometime mid-century. This medical center was closed down in 2007. It once housed over 100 beds and had state-of-the-art medical equipment. Unfortunately, this hospital met its demise and was demolished late 2018.

A long dark hallway leading into the hospital.

Most of the rooms still had beds that had endured the test of time. All of them possessed varying degrees of decay from slightly newer looking to being completely overtaken by rust.

This couch sits untouched in the waiting room of the nursery.

Another image of the nursery with teddy bear wallpaper and a shattered viewing window.

Above: Operating room #1 was located in the back of the building and was smaller than the rest.

Opposite: In operating room #2, all that was left were the lights and the doctor's chair.

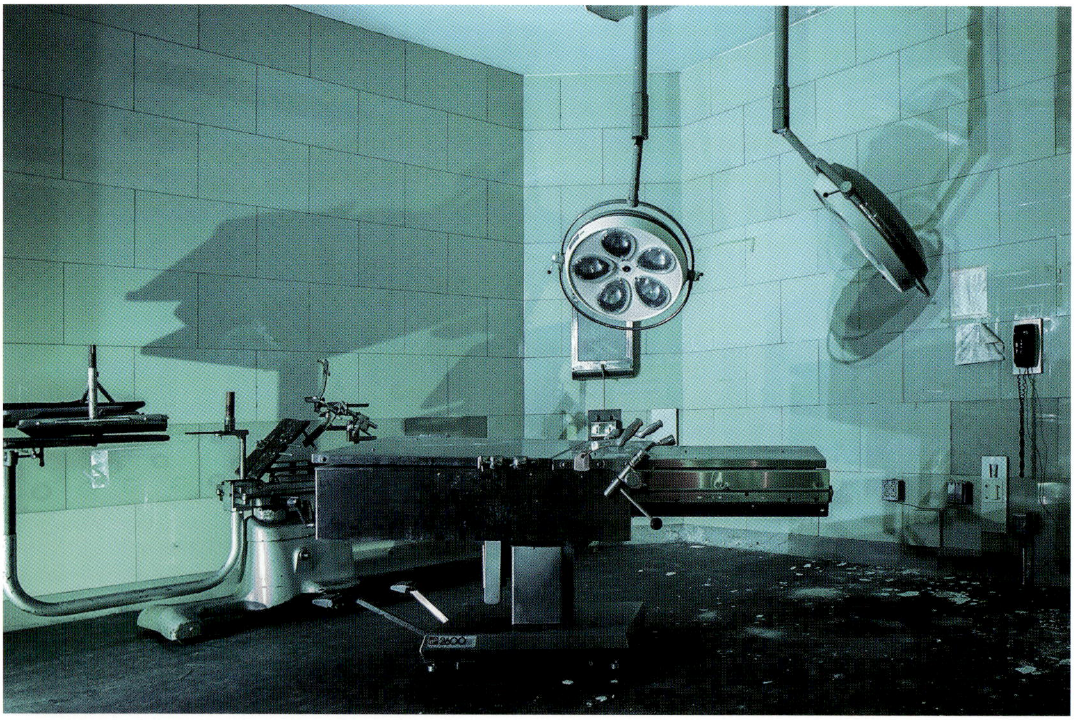

Operating room #3 was full of all sorts of medical items. Here sits an original operating table, lights, and other medical devices.

The nurses' station was located right outside of the operating rooms.

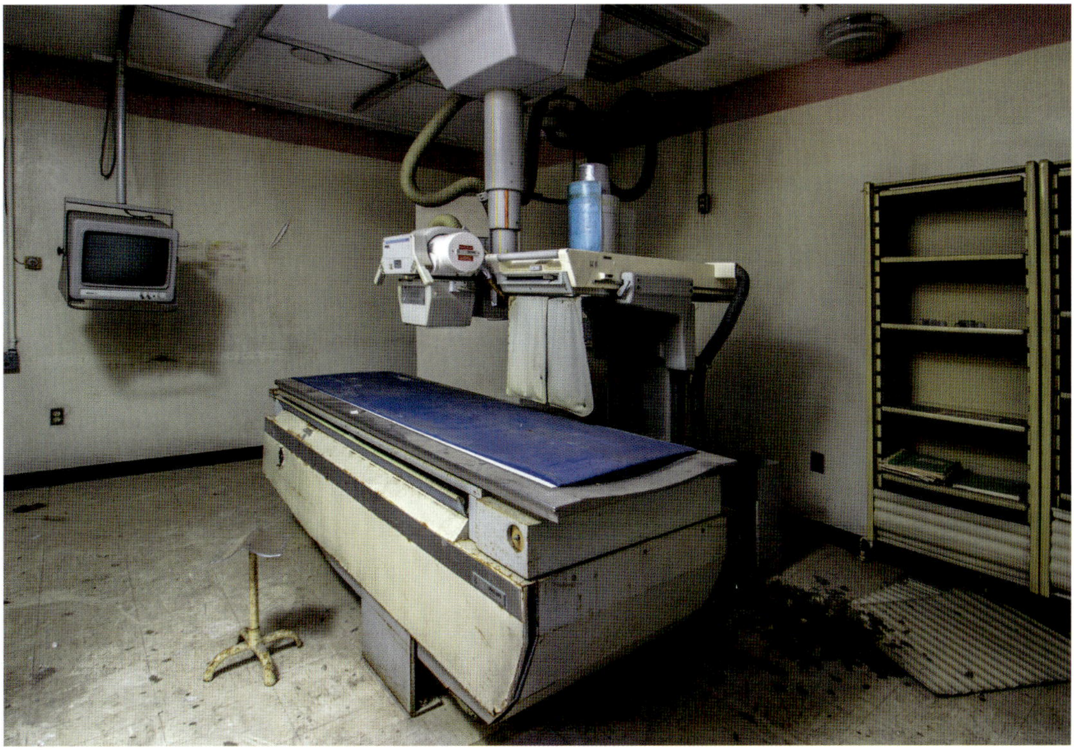

The x-ray table was once located in the basement of the Palestine Hospital.

The overly photographed wheelchair in the hallway. This same image was taken by the majority of explorers that had visited this location.

Many of the original machines were scattered throughout the hospital corridors and remained intact before the arrival of vandals, thieves, and ultimately the demolition crew.

This incubator sits in a deserted room filled with medical equipment.

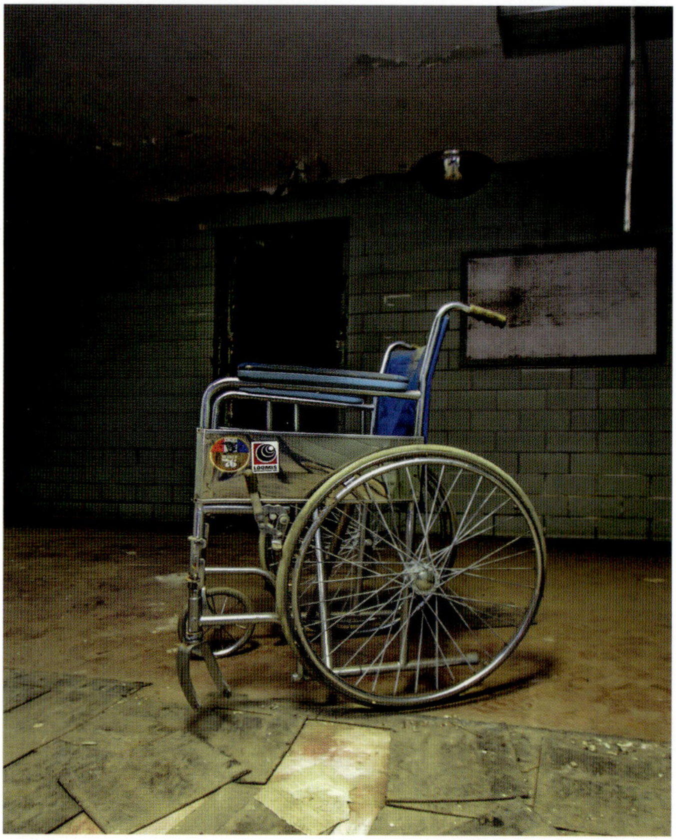

Above: The paperwork of previous patients remained. We found EKGs and other health records that had been discarded by the staff.

Left: Another wheelchair sits in solitude. This one happened to be in the basement.

4

SCHOOLS

Rumor has it that this red brick school was built on a cemetery in 1913 and was abandoned in 1957. The field surrounding it is full of devil's thorns and the walls are full of beehives.

Population change, shortage of funding, and lack of enrolment often cause the closing of Texas schools. Sometimes, entire school districts are closed by the state. Schools built in the early-nineteenth century up until modern day can be found dispersed around the state.

Above: The upper floor of this school still contained the original seating.

Opposite: The majority of the walls had beehives and a surreal constant buzzing could be heard.

The main hallway of the school is a good example of natural decay and doesn't really show signs of vandals.

One of the school gyms we came across was full of plastic ball pit balls. There were hundreds of these strewn about.

This is a night shot of a cafeteria in a South Dallas school. Shortly after this was taken, all of the tables and chairs were stolen.

Above: School lockers generally fill the hallways of these closed schools.

Opposite: This disintegrating school in Greenville was built in the 1900s. It was one of three segregated schools at the time.

This box of checkers sits in the back of an elementary school.

Daycare at a Catholic school. This place had the stench of death in the air. We came across a couple of dead animals, but the pungent smell seemed to come from elsewhere. We looked around but were never able to find the source.

The nursery was next door to the daycare in the Catholic school. The entire place is covered in black mold.

With the extreme heat and humidity in Texas, unmaintained gym floors don't stand a chance. This wood floor had been destroyed in just a couple of years from lack of care.

The classrooms are still occupied with desks organized and ready for class.

This row of trophies was left in a run-down school in East Texas.

A once used abacus sits alone in a math classroom.

The auditorium of a large Dallas school. This school was closed due to lack of enrollment and funding.

The choir room of a large school in Dallas.

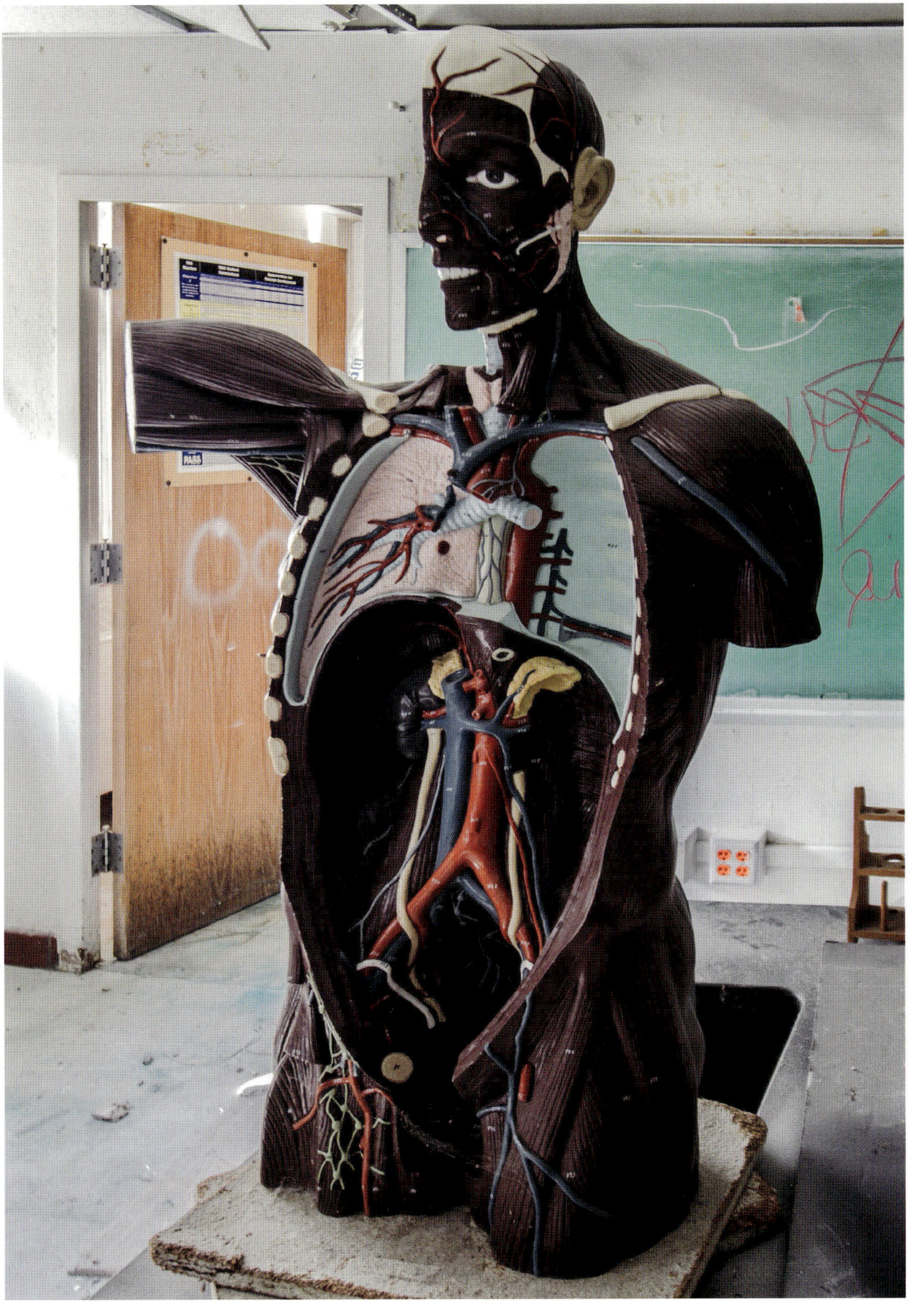

There were a few of these anatomical dummies left in some of the classrooms.

A well placed piece of graffiti in a boy's gym.

The main staircase leading to the upper floors in a Dallas school.

The hallway of the Central Ward School in Dennison, Texas. This building has since been condemned by the city.

This lonesome chair sits in front of a textured brick wall.

An original corroded hand towel dispenser in the Central Ward School.

The auditorium in a Texarkana school. The roof had mostly collapsed and is now home to a large predatory bird. Needless to say, the bird was not happy we were there and made it obvious that he wanted us to leave.

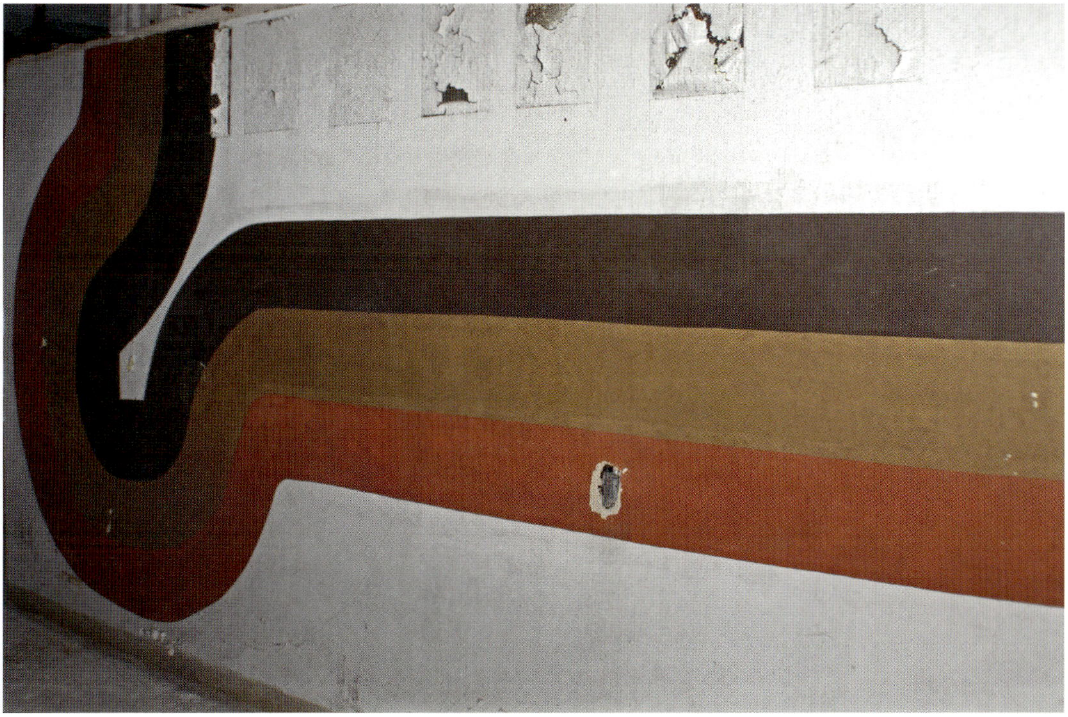

A decorative graphic inside the Dallas High School in the middle of downtown Dallas. This location has since been renovated into lofts, apartments, and retail shops.

Some schools are used to teach farming practices to help shape the future farmers of tomorrow.

An exterior shot of the Gilliland School.

The Gilliland School

The Gilliland School was built in the 1930s. When the school was first opened, they taught all grades from kindergarten to 12th grade. After World War II, it transitioned to be just an elementary school. The town of Gilliland never had a large population, and by the year 2000, it was mostly deserted. This decrepit school building resides in the middle of a field while nature reclaims it.

What's left of the bathroom.

The school had a full-size gym complete with a basketball court and stage for school plays and performances.

Most of the classrooms are in disrepair and are gradually falling apart.

The main corridor of the school is barely distinguishable anymore as natural deterioration takes over.

A chemical bucket forgotten in a hallway.

Another classroom that appears to be on its last leg. There is not much that remains besides the weathered chalkboard.

Today's children will never understand old school encyclopedias.

Pianos often meet their demise wasting away in empty classrooms.

It appears that someone may have lived here at one point.

There are many books that litter the floor from the elementary students that once attended.

The front door has become overgrown with trees.

A busted volleyball.

The remains of rusty playground equipment can be found in the overgrown field behind the school.

Once used furniture that has been lost to time.

There are many dangers in doing what we do. Rural Texas is a hotbed for snakes. This school is especially known for its rattler population. During the summer, it is a snake haven. Thankfully, we spotted this guy before anyone stepped on it.

The view of the back of the gym.

5

INDUSTRIAL

This image was taken from the office of the North Texas Steel Company in Ft. Worth, Texas. It has been demolished and the warehouse has turned into a homeless camp.

The Lone Star State has plenty of room to accommodate its industries. With an endless amount of land to work with, many towns were built up around industrial factories. With the huge amount of space Texas has to offer, when a company moves or closes, the property is usually just left to rot. Power plants, refineries, factories, and a number of other industrial locations are scattered within the entire state.

Waste tanks from a pig slaughterhouse in Richardson.

The killing floor at the slaughterhouse of a well-known sausage manufacturer in North Texas.

W. S. Dickey Clay Manufacturing Company located in Texarkana.

The main warehouse of this brick factory was filled with discarded tires.

The skybridge and offices of Central Freight in Irving, Texas.

The view from inside the skybridge. Both the offices and skybridge have been demolished.

The logistic docks for Central Freight. Currently this area still stands but is threatened by redevelopment.

The loading docks of a desolate cement factory.

A sunset reflection in a pool of wastewater outside of this industrial giant.

A fisheye view of the stairwell located in the plant.

A bird's eye view of what has become an industrial wasteland.

There is a ridiculous number of pipes that lead through this refinery. It truly felt like a man-made jungle.

A tunnel completely constructed of pipes.

For years, one of the most notorious industrial locations was the Swift Meat Packing Plant near the stockyards in Ft. Worth, Texas. This historic location was demolished a couple of years ago. Only a small portion that was used for a TV show now remains.

Inside the T & P Warehouse in downtown Ft. Worth, Texas. Pretty much every floor looked the same, with a few small differences on each level. The city has recently replaced all of the windows in this building.

A reflection shot from the flooded Baker McQueen in Marshall, Texas.

The roof of the Texas and Pacific Warehouse has little concrete huts all along the top of it. The view from up here is amazing.

A unique shot of the South Side Silo that is also situated in Ft. Worth. This place has been known to be full of aggressive homeless drug addicts.

The stairs inside the South Side Silo. This location smelled worse than any other place we have been to.

This is the Echo Lake incinerator, in 2009, before it was completely covered in graffiti. The incinerator is in a lower income area and is a frequent hangout spot for the local gangs and teenagers.

The inside of this place is pierced with bullet holes and riddled with graffiti. The land was recently purchased by new owners who have plans to revamp the area.

The control panel inside the abandoned TXU Power Plant in Ft. Worth.

This structure was full of rickety steep staircases leading to upper floors, where you can find giant windows everywhere. Driving by it, you can see that most of the windows have been shattered.

The last remains of a cinder block factory in South Dallas. This place was used for a few different purposes. It was a spot for paintball, graffiti, and ultimately for vandals to scrap everything left standing.

Once again, we just wanted to reiterate the fact that we do not condone trespassing or breaking the law in any way. We have been able to obtain legal access to many of the properties photographed. This hobby isn't for everyone and great risks can be involved. Please check out our social media sites listed in the front of the book. Also, keep an eye out for our second edition *Abandoned South Texas*.

BIBLIOGRAPHY

Wikipedia Contributors. (2018, October 29). Baker Hotel (Mineral Wells, Texas). In *Wikipedia, The Free Encyclopedia*. Retrieved October 30, 2018, from: https://en.wikipedia.org/w/index.php?title=Baker_Hotel_(Mineral_Wells,_Texas)&oldid=866352905.

Wikipedia Contributors. (2018, January 17). Texoma Medical Center. In *Wikipedia, The Free Encyclopedia*. Retrieved October 30, 2018, from: https://en.wikipedia.org/w/index.php?title=Texoma_Medical_Center&oldid=820872342.

Wikipedia Contributors. (2018, August 12). Indian Gap, Texas. In *Wikipedia, The Free Encyclopedia*. Retrieved October 30, 2018, from: https://en.wikipedia.org/w/index.php?title=Indian_Gap,_Texas&oldid=854644980.